SPEED ZONE
SUPERFAST ROCKETS

by Alicia Z. Klepeis

pogo

Ideas for Parents and Teachers

Pogo Books let children practice reading informational text while introducing them to nonfiction features such as headings, labels, sidebars, maps, and diagrams, as well as a table of contents, glossary, and index.

Carefully leveled text with a strong photo match offers early fluent readers the support they need to succeed.

Before Reading

- "Walk" through the book and point out the various nonfiction features. Ask the student what purpose each feature serves.
- Look at the glossary together. Read and discuss the words.

Read the Book

- Have the child read the book independently.
- Invite him or her to list questions that arise from reading.

After Reading

- Discuss the child's questions. Talk about how he or she might find answers to those questions.
- Prompt the child to think more. Ask: What did you know about rockets before reading this book? What more would you like to learn about them?

Pogo Books are published by Jump!
5357 Penn Avenue South
Minneapolis, MN 55419
www.jumplibrary.com

Copyright © 2022 Jump!
International copyright reserved in all countries. No part of this book may be reproduced in any form without written permission from the publisher.

Library of Congress Cataloging-in-Publication Data

Names: Klepeis, Alicia, 1971- author.
Title: Superfast rockets / by Alicia Z. Klepeis.
Description: Minneapolis, MN: Jump!, Inc., [2022]
Series: Speed zone
Includes index. | Audience: Ages 7-10.
Identifiers: LCCN 2020055119 (print)
LCCN 2020055120 (ebook)
ISBN 9781645279679 (hardcover)
ISBN 9781645279686 (paperback)
ISBN 9781645279693 (ebook)
Subjects: LCSH: Rockets (Aeronautics)—Juvenile literature.
Classification: LCC TL782.5 .K558 2022 (print)
LCC TL782.5 (ebook) | DDC 629.4–dc23
LC record available at https://lccn.loc.gov/2020055119
LC ebook record available at https://lccn.loc.gov/2020055120

Editor: Eliza Leahy
Designer: Molly Ballanger

Photo Credits: Lone Pine/Shutterstock, cover; Mikephotos/Dreamstime, 1; NASA, 3, 4, 5, 10-11, 12-13, 16; Alexandr Yurtchenko/Dreamstime, 6-7; iStock, 8; Science Collection/Alamy, 9; Babuhka Boa/Shutterstock, 14-15; Dima Zel/Shutterstock, 17; muratart/Shutterstock, 18-19; Nick Servian/robertharding/SuperStock, 20-21; 3DSculptor/iStock, 23.

Printed in the United States of America at Corporate Graphics in North Mankato, Minnesota.

TABLE OF CONTENTS

CHAPTER 1
Blastoff! 4

CHAPTER 2
Traveling in Space 8

CHAPTER 3
Speedy Rockets 16

ACTIVITIES & TOOLS
Try This! 22
Glossary 23
Index 24
To Learn More 24

CHAPTER 1

BLASTOFF!

Ten... Nine... Eight... A rocket is on a **launch pad**. It is about to blast off into outer space!

Bright flames burst from the rocket. It soars into the sky. In just over two minutes, it will already be 34 miles (55 kilometers) up. It goes more than 5,450 miles (8,771 km) per hour! It will gain even more speed as it travels.

Like all **engines**, a rocket engine burns fuel. This creates hot gas. The engine pushes the gas out the bottom. This pushes the rocket up. This **force** is called **thrust**. It works against **gravity** and **drag**.

TAKE A LOOK!

How does a rocket's thrust work against gravity? Take a look!

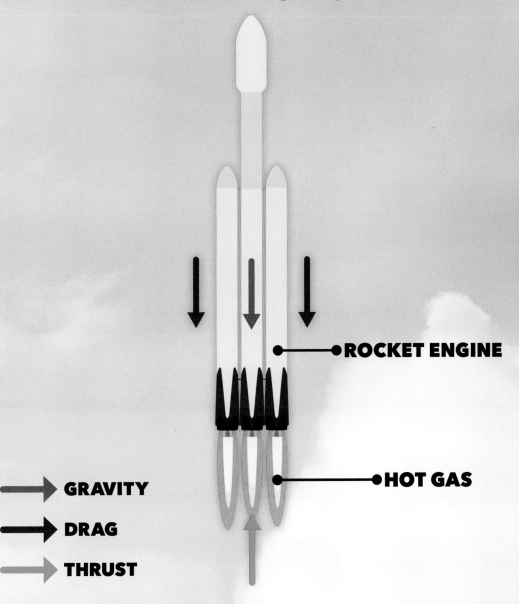

GRAVITY

DRAG

THRUST

ROCKET ENGINE

HOT GAS

CHAPTER 2

TRAVELING IN SPACE

How does a rocket travel in space? The answer is **stages**. These are sections of the rocket. Each stage has its own engine or engines. The engines in the first stage send the rocket into the sky.

When that stage runs out of fuel, it breaks off from the rocket. Why? This gets rid of extra weight. The rocket can go faster. Stages fall into the ocean or burn up in Earth's **atmosphere**. Some are **recovered**.

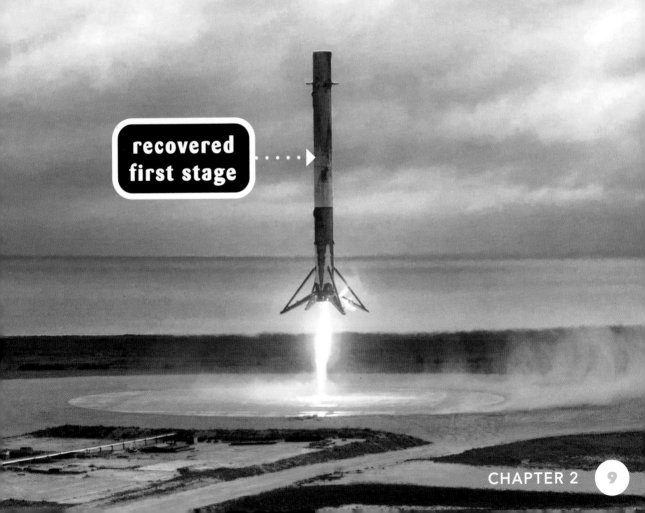

recovered first stage

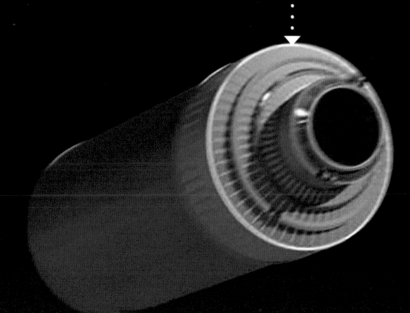

stage

Then the second stage starts. Another engine sends the rocket farther. This process keeps going until the rocket gets to its destination. Many rockets have three stages. Some have as many as five!

DID YOU KNOW?

What do rockets carry? Some carry **satellites**. Others carry astronauts. They can even carry Mars **rovers**!

Rocket frames are built with very strong materials. But they have to be light. Why? Lighter rockets need less power to gain speed.

fin

Rockets are often narrow. This shape is **aerodynamic**. It reduces drag.

Some rockets have fins at the bottom. They help keep the rockets steady.

CHAPTER 3

SPEEDY ROCKETS

Atlas V

What are some of the speediest rockets? The Atlas V launched the New Horizons spacecraft toward Pluto in 2006. Its launch speed was the fastest ever. It went about 36,400 miles (58,580 km) per hour!

Space Launch System

Another speedy rocket is the Space Launch System. It will launch the Orion and its astronauts to the moon. Orion will reach 24,500 miles (39,429 km) per hour.

The Delta IV Heavy rocket sent the Parker Solar **Probe** (PSP) into space. The PSP will be the fastest spacecraft ever. It will reach about 430,000 miles (692,018 km) per hour. At that speed, you could go from Washington, D.C., to Tokyo in under one minute!

DID YOU KNOW?

Just four days after launch, the PSP traveled 39,000 miles (62,764 km) per hour. It had traveled 2.9 million miles (4.7 million km) from Earth in that time!

Parker
Solar Probe

We want to travel farther into space. Rockets will need to go even faster. **Engineers** keep designing. How fast do you think rockets will go?

DID YOU KNOW?

Scientists are studying **nuclear**-powered engines. These could produce more thrust. More thrust could mean faster and farther trips.

ACTIVITIES & TOOLS

MAKE A BALLOON ROCKET

Build a balloon rocket and see how far it goes with this fun activity!

What You Need:

- a 10-foot (3-meter) piece of string
- a straw
- a balloon (Hint: Longer-shaped balloons work best.)
- tape

❶ Tie one end of the string to a support such as a doorknob, table leg, or chair.

❷ Pull the other end of the string through the straw.

❸ Pull the string tight. Tie this end to a different support in the room.

❹ Blow up your balloon. Do not tie it. Keep the end of the balloon pinched tightly. Tape the balloon to the straw so it sits beneath it.

❺ Let go of the end of the balloon. Watch your rocket fly!

GLOSSARY

aerodynamic: Designed to move through the air easily and quickly.

atmosphere: The mixture of gases that surrounds a planet.

drag: The force that slows motion, action, or advancement.

engineers: People who are specially trained to design and build machines or large structures.

engines: Machines that make things move by using gasoline, steam, or another energy source.

force: Any action that produces, stops, or changes the shape or movement of an object.

gravity: The force that pulls things toward the center of Earth and keeps them from floating away.

launch pad: The platform from which a rocket is sent into space.

nuclear: Of or having to do with the energy created by splitting atoms.

probe: A spacecraft designed to explore or examine its environment.

recovered: Got something back that was lost or taken away.

rovers: Vehicles that can drive over rough terrain, often in space.

satellites: Spacecraft that are sent into orbit around Earth, the moon, or another planet.

stages: Sections of rockets that have their own engines and are discarded when their fuel is used up.

thrust: The forward force produced by the engine of a rocket.

INDEX

aerodynamic 15

astronauts 11, 17

Atlas V 16

atmosphere 9

Delta IV Heavy 18

drag 6, 7, 15

engineers 21

engines 6, 7, 8, 11, 21

fins 15

frames 12

fuel 6, 9

gas 6, 7

gravity 6, 7

materials 12

moon 17

New Horizons 16

Orion 17

Parker Solar Probe 18

Pluto 16

rovers 11

satellites 11

Space Launch System 17

stages 8, 9, 11

thrust 6, 7, 21

Tokyo 18

Washington, D.C. 18

TO LEARN MORE

Finding more information is as easy as 1, 2, 3.

1 Go to www.factsurfer.com

2 Enter "superfastrockets" into the search box.

3 Choose your book to see a list of websites.

FACT SURFER